Dedicated to:

Savannah, Marisa, Olivia, Taylor, Summer, Jason and Shilah

for

sticking by each other during a really hard time. I am thankful we were together and God gave us the gift of friendship.

Written by: Abigail Gartland

I am also known as St. John the Evangelist. That means I spent my life spreading the word of God.

I was born near Galilee just a few years after Jesus.

When I was a young man, Jesus asked me to follow Him along with my brother, St. James.

James and I spent a lot of time following and learning from Jesus. He called the two of us "Sons of Thunder."

Jesus gave us this nickname because we were passionate and loyal to His teachings. We had a burning fire in our hearts for Him.

One day, Jesus was approached by a man named Jairus. He said that his young daughter had passed away.

We followed Jarius to his house. We saw that his daughter had passed away in her bed.

Everyone was so sad, but Jesus said that she was not dead; she was just sleeping.

We were very confused, but Jesus put His head down and prayed. He said, "Little girl, arise."

Suddenly, the little girl opened her eyes and sat up.

Jesus had performed a miracle and brought her back to life!

We saw many miracles during the life of Jesus.

Jesus was soon crucified and died for our sins.

I was the only one of Jesus' friends who did not leave His side, and I stayed with His mother, Mary.

Before Jesus died, He told me that Mary was now my mother, too. I took care of her for the rest of her life.

spent the rest of my life sharing the word of God, and I wrote the stories of Jesus' life. I am one of the four gospel writers.

Do you want to be more like me?

You can celebrate my feast day with me on December 27th.

I am the patron saint of love, friendship and authors!

I pray for you every day of your life.

St. John the Apostle, pray for us!

pyright:

part: © PentoolPixie © LimeandKiwiDesigns
ensed purchased: 1/10/2024

About the Author

Abigail Gartland

I love the saints and I love my faith. The idea for sharing the stories of the saints with little ones came when my dear friend were expecting their first baby. I wanted t create something as unique and special as our friendship. Each book is dedicated to very special people and groups who have enriched my faith in different ways. I am blessed to write these stories and appreciate the unending support of my family and friends. When I am not writing, am a middle school teacher. I hope you enjoy these stories. I pray for each and every person who opens one of my books to learn more about the saints.

Abbie

www.ingramcontent.com/pod-product-compliance
Lightning Source LLC
LaVergne TN
LVHW051041070526
838201LV00067B/4886